Contents

Acknowledgements
Thanks to Bob Blakeborough and Steve Haynes for their assistance with the text, and to Charles Nolan and Tom Gilvarry jnr for taking part in the photographic session. Thanks also to Tom Gilvarry snr of Moy Table Enterprises Ltd for his contribution to this book, and to Mick King of The Golden Lion public house in London Colney for the loan of part of his pub!
Photographs by Chris Lobina of Sporting Pictures (UK) Ltd.
Illustrations by 1-11 line-art

The British Association of Pool Table Operators, c/o Moy House, 176 High Street, London Colney, Hertfordshire AL2 1JY.

Note Throughout the book players and officials are referred to individually as 'he'. This should, of course, be taken to mean 'he or she' where appropriate.

Foreword

Know The Game Pool has been compiled under the guidance of The British Association of Pool Table Operators. BAPTO was formed in 1975 in order to harmonise the activities of those involved in the supply of pool tables to the licensed trade. It is responsible for the promotion of the game and for the standardisation of the rules of pool in the UK.

Though a commercial body, BAPTO has a vested interest in the development of pool and in the popularity and strength of the game. BAPTO is delighted with the progress that has been made over the last two decades, and wishes to thank all those who have supported the association and its work.

Introduction

Pool is a game of skill and tactics in which the novice and intermediate player are rarely embarrassed even when playing an experienced and skilful opponent.

As with all sports and games, expertise and a clear knowledge of the game is gained only with plenty of practice. It is acknowledged that no book can guarantee instant success, but hopefully this publication and your dedication to the game will get you moving in the right direction. The fact that you are reading this book shows that you have the correct attitude to improve your game, but only time and dedication will determine to what level you aspire.

Work at fully understanding the game and the skills required, rather than copying others who may be very successful but who may have acquired over a period of time a series of bad habits. Bad habits are easy to acquire but difficult to get rid of, hence the tips and hints provided in this book. They are intended to help you improve your game, to avoid bad habits, but at the same time to help you appreciate and practise the best of what you see in others.

Know The Game Pool is predominantly geared towards the most popular game in the UK – 8-ball pool – but you will find a section on several simple fun games which can be played on a pool table. Pool techniques apply to all of these games.

The game

The game is played by two individuals, or two teams usually not exceeding two players per team. In the event of a team game, the partners have alternate 'visits' to the table.

The game is played with 16 balls. The white ball, known as the 'cue ball', is slightly smaller than the other balls – 14 object balls and the 8-ball black. The object balls are seven balls numbered 1 to 7 and seven numbered 9 to 15, or seven balls of one colour (usually red) and seven of another colour (usually yellow).

The purpose of the game is for a player to pocket all of his object balls and then the 8-ball black. Until the game is under way, a player's group of object balls is not yet established – this is explained later.

Equipment

The table

Pool tables vary in size and usually have overall external measurements of 6 ft × 3 ft 6 in (1.8 m × 1.06 m), 7 ft × 4 ft (2.1 m × 1.2 m) or 8 ft × 4 ft 6 in (2.4 m × 1.4 m). The actual playing surface is less than this, so a 7 ft × 4 ft (2.1 m × 1.2 m) table would have a playing size of 6 ft × 3 ft (1.8 m × 0.9 m). In other words, the playing surface is in most cases 1 ft (0.3 m) less in both length and width. The height of a pool table is 31–34 in (79–86 cm).

The playing surface of the table, known as the 'bed', is normally made of slate and is covered traditionally by a wool, nylon or a wool/nylon mix cloth. The 'nap' of this cloth runs from the 'D' end of the table to the bottom cushion. A 'gabardine' or napless nylon cloth is used occasionally to provide a very hard-wearing cloth, arguably creating a faster game, but with less control, particularly of the cue ball. Although most tables are covered in a green cloth, other colours are available and are used to suit the cosmetic or decorative needs of a location.

The bed of the table is surrounded by six cushions and six pockets – *see* fig. 1. The cushions are constructed of a wooden frame to which the flat-faced rubber cushions are attached. Then the construction is covered in the same material as the bed of the table. Pool tables have flat-faced cushions so that the bounce of the object balls, which are normally 2 in (5 cm) in diameter, and the cue ball, 1.9 in (4.8 cm) in diameter, is consistent. The size of the pockets should be 1.6 times the diameter of an object ball at the point where the ball drops off the table.

The playing area bears certain markings, indicated in fig. 1. The 8-ball spot is located at the intersection of the diagonals of the central and bottom corner pockets. The 'string line' runs across the table, one-fifth of the distance from the top cushion to the bottom cushion. On the string line a 'D' is drawn towards the top cushion, the diameter being equal to one-third of the width of the table. Some tables are marked with the string line right across the table: this is acceptable and also accommodates other games which can be played on pool tables.

▲ *Lighting canopy*

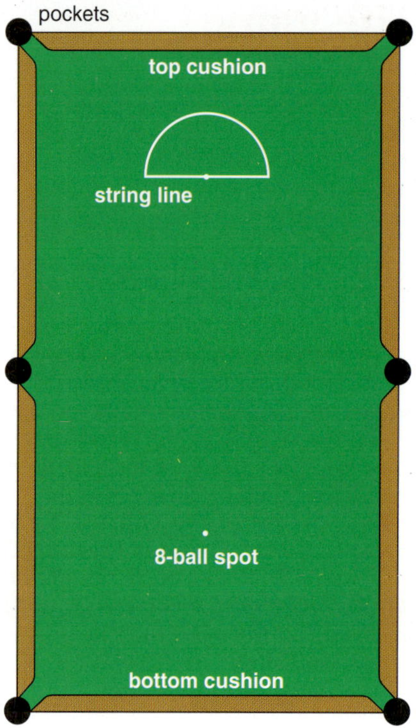

▲► *Fig. 1 The pool table*

It is desirable that there is ample room around the table to play a shot at every point with a standard size cue. (Very short cues are available to enable shots to be played from obstructed locations.) Most important is that the table is perfectly level, so it is particularly undesirable for a table to be placed in a position which is not permanent. However, if there is no alternative the use of a purpose-made pool trolley will assist moving the table and give a greater chance of returning it to exactly the same, level position.

A table needs to be maintained in good condition. The playing surface should be brushed daily with a soft nylon or horse hair brush, in the direction of the nap – from the 'D' to the bottom cushion. A cloth made of wool or wool/nylon should be ironed regularly, again in the direction of the nap. Before ironing, the cloth should be brushed and cleaned with a damp cloth to lift any surface grit and dirt. The pocket liners should be checked regularly to ensure that they are seated firmly in the pockets, and it is also a good idea to check the shoes into which the balls drop and all other cosmetic fitments.

Players should look after the table by ensuring that it is clean and used in a careful manner with cues that are in good condition. Don't smoke over the table and, most important of all, don't toss or drop coins on to the bed of the table – coins are the most common cause of small cuts appearing on the playing surface. Use a piece of cloth on which to rack up the balls so that the sweat which is transmitted from your hands to the triangle does not finish up on the bed cloth.

▲ *A middle pocket*

▲ *A corner pocket*

▲ *Brushing the cloth*

Cues

Pool cues are made of various woods, such as redwood, maple, willow, sandalwood and ash. Most cues supplied in licensed premises are cheap softwood versions imported from the Far East. These are normally 48 in (122 cm) long for a 6 ft table, and 54–57 in (137–145 cm) long for longer tables. The circumference at the handle end is approximately 3.5–4 in (9–10 cm).

Cues are normally weighted with a metal weight at the thick end of the cue, and the tip is mounted in a metal or plastic ferrule. Cue tips are usually 0.43–0.47 in (11–12 mm) in diameter. Keen players may wish to invest in a higher quality hardwood cue of their own. Those that do this tend to select a smaller tip size, 0.31–0.39 in (8–10 mm) in diameter.

It is desirable to dust the tip of the cue with chalk before you play, thus ensuring smooth contact with the cue ball and hopefully preventing shots being miscued.

As the cues that are supplied with pool tables are for general use, unfortunately they are abused and quickly become damaged. The novice player is likely to be using such cues and so he should always ensure that there are no sharp edges, particularly around the tip end of the cue because this would dig into the playing surface. If it catches and tears the cloth, this can be a very expensive accident!

Cues should always be stored in a cool, dry place, certainly not near radiators or in damp conditions because this will cause warping of the wood. A simple method of checking that a cue is straight is to roll it on the table. If it rolls evenly then it is still true, but if it jumps like a wheel with a hole not in the centre then you know something is wrong. It is fair to say that many experienced players use a cue which has become warped over the years, and do so quite successfully. So while it may not be desirable to play with a cue that is warped, it is not necessarily a disadvantage.

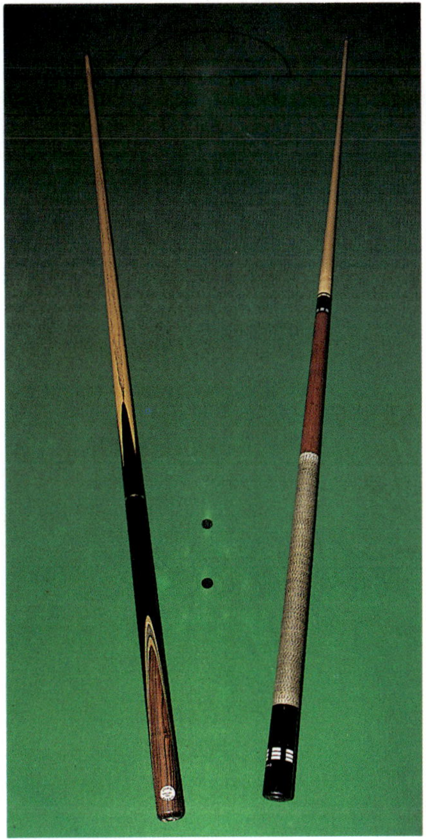

Keen players may wish to invest in a high ► quality hardwood cue of their own

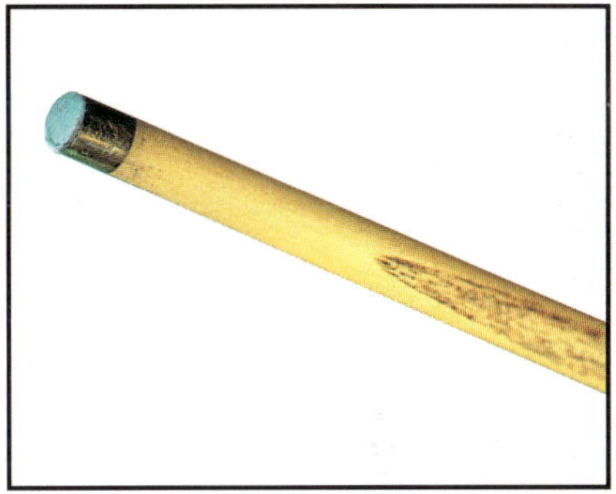

▲ *Cue tip*

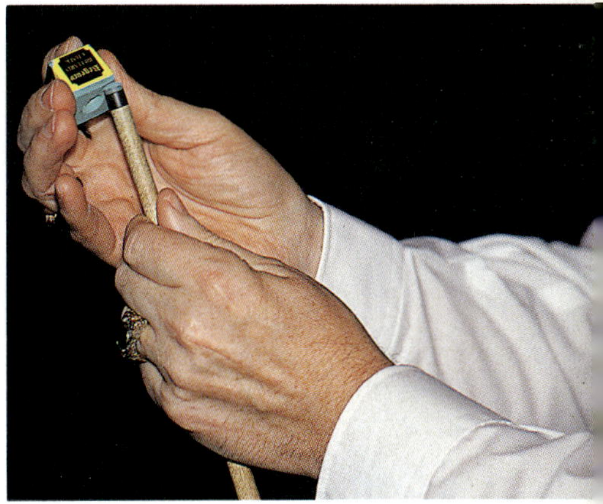

▲ *Chalking the tip of the cue*

The black 8-ball

The cue ball

The balls

There are 16 balls in total. They are usually made of phenolic resin, and all but the cue ball are usually 2 in (5 cm) in diameter. The cue ball is slightly smaller and is plain white. The other balls, the object balls, are traditionally numbered 1–15; number 8, known as the '8-ball', is black, and the others are so coloured as to divide them into two even groups. The original rules state that numbers 1–7 should be plain colours and numbers 9–15 striped, and

the two groups are commonly known as the 'spots' or 'solids' and the 'stripes'. However, the game is now increasingly played with unnumbered coloured balls, e.g. seven red, seven yellow, one black and a white cue ball. This makes the lay of the balls easier to see and plan, eliminates the occasional mistake in identifying balls, and makes play much easier for spectators to follow.

The balls should be kept clean and smooth by an occasional polish with a soft rag.

The rack

The rack is made of plastic or wood and is in the shape of a triangle. It is used at the start of the game as an aid to placing the balls in their correct positions (*see* page 21).

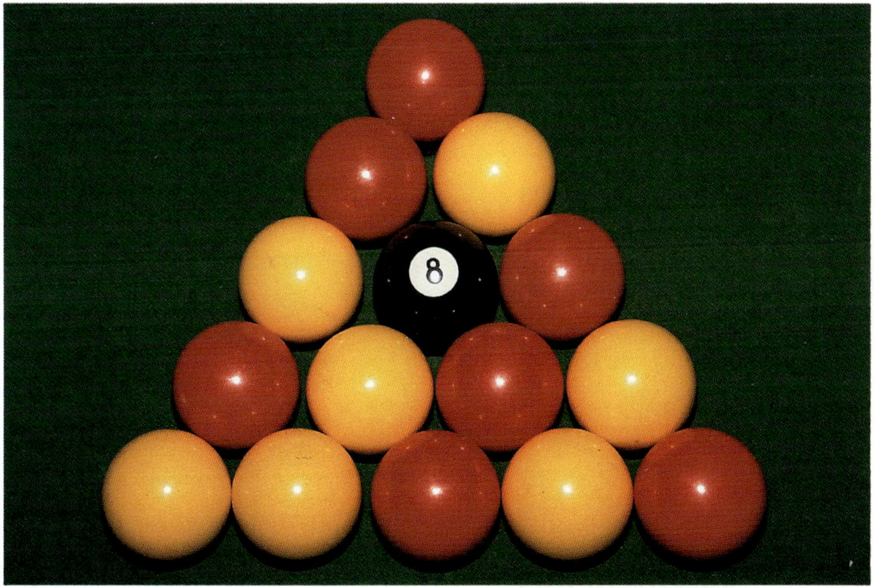

◀ *'Spots and stripes'*

▲ *Unnumbered, coloured balls*

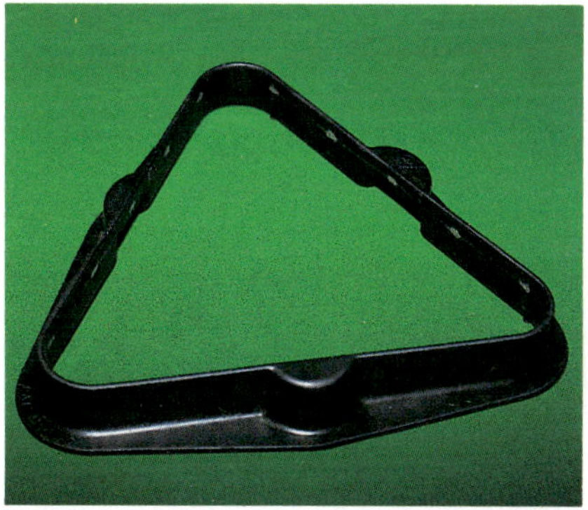

▲ *Plastic rack*

Object of the game

The object of the game is absolutely straightforward – you hit the white cue ball (shared by both sides) and with it try to knock into the pockets your own seven balls, then legally pot the black (8-ball). It does not matter in which order you pocket your seven balls – the numbers, if they have them, are irrelevant in 8-ball pool.

Learning the basics

Holding the cue

Find the point of balance of the cue and grasp the cue lightly but securely a few inches behind this point (i.e. further towards you). Experimentation will quickly determine the most comfortable point of grip on any cue.

▲ *Holding the cue, view from above*

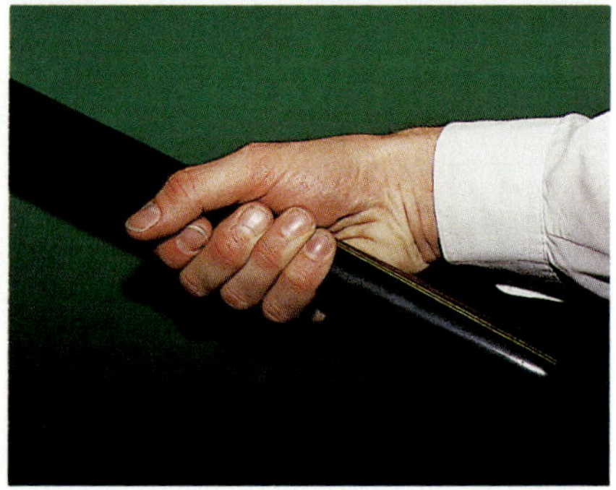

▲ *Holding the cue, view from the side*

The bridge

Next, place the other hand (the left hand for right-handers) flat on the pool table, fingers pointing away from you. Leaving the heel of the hand on the table, draw the fingers back, bending them and leaving the tips touching the table.

Raise the thumb high, to form a 'V' between the thumb and forefinger knuckle, into which the shaft of the cue may be rested. By bringing the tips of the little finger and forefinger slightly behind the other two, you create a firm base ready for the time when the heel of the hand must be raised in order to make the cue strike the cue ball at a higher point. This position is also necessary in order to pass the cue over obstructing object balls.

You have now learned how to form a 'bridge', and this is used to rest the cue on by the vast majority of players, with perhaps some minor personal touches. The importance of the bridge is often underestimated, and many an otherwise excellent player will lose consistently through having a rickety bridge and mis-cueing relatively simple strokes.

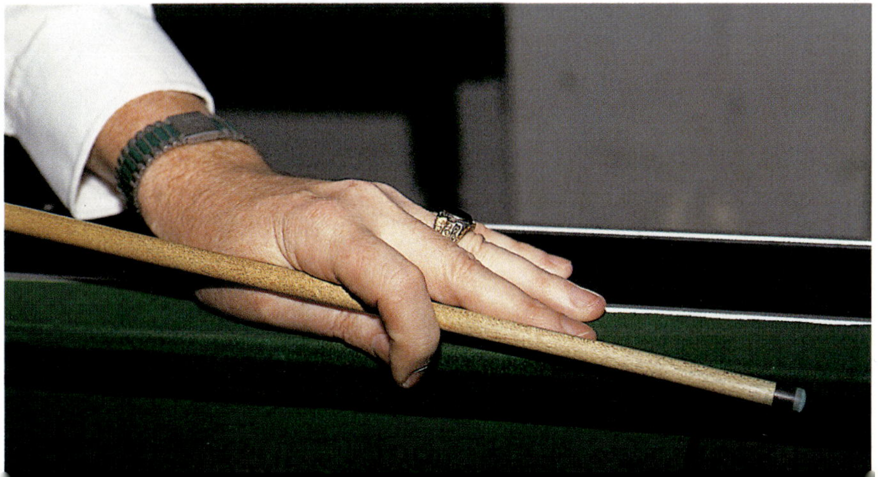

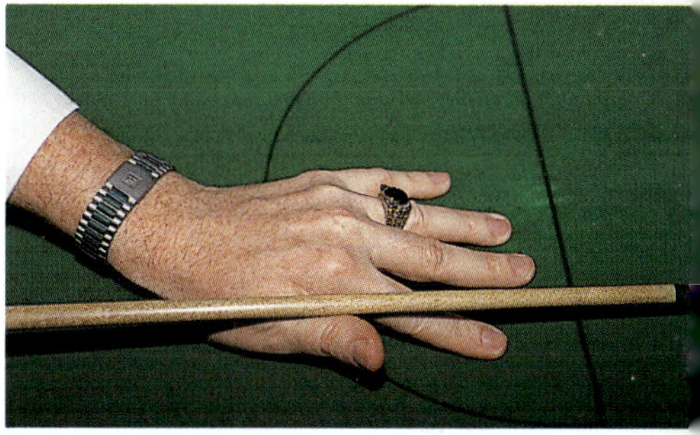

▲ *Conventional bridge*

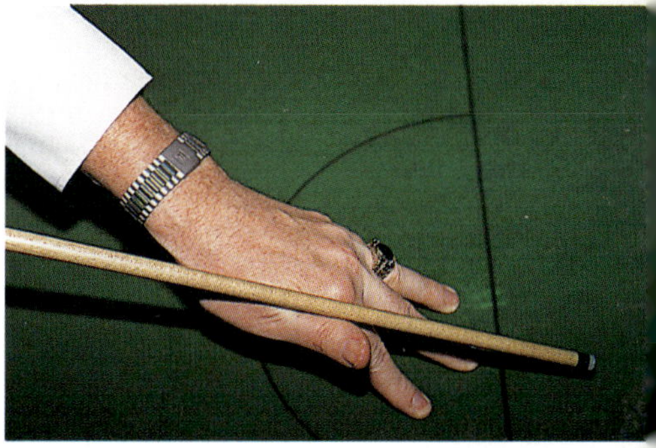

▲ *Raised bridge*

◄ *Where it is impractical to form a conventional bridge, the hand can be shaped in a comfortable manner to support the cue*

Stance

To practise the correct stance, first place one ball in the 'D' at the head of the table. Stand at a 45° angle to the table, with your bridge hand nearest the table, feet comfortably apart.

With your feet in the same position, pivot round until you are facing the cue ball. Lean forwards to place the bridge hand in a position so that the cue will rest on it, with the tip almost touching and able to strike the cue ball.

Keeping the rear leg straight, bend forwards to bring the chin down until it almost touches the cue. Some players prefer to touch the cue lightly with the chin to give them a greater awareness of alignment with the cue ball.

You can now look forwards along the cue at the cue ball. Keep both eyes open. It is not like sighting a rifle over a long distance – the three-dimensional effect of both eyes is more accurate and will give you better alignment of cue and cue ball to target.

Adjust your foot and leg positions until your stance is comfortable and steady. Now move the cue backwards and forwards towards the centre of the cue ball to ensure a smooth, straight, flowing movement. This is perhaps best achieved by locking the upper part of the cue arm into a position with the shoulder over the cue and the elbow in alignment with the shoulder, bridge hand and cue ball. Only the forearm is then allowed to move, swinging backwards and forwards in a smooth rhythm, carrying the cue straight towards its target. Many of the most accomplished players may be observed using this technique to eliminate 'hooking' the cue arm.

▲ *Looking along the cue at the cue ball; arms parallel to the cue; body equally balanced*

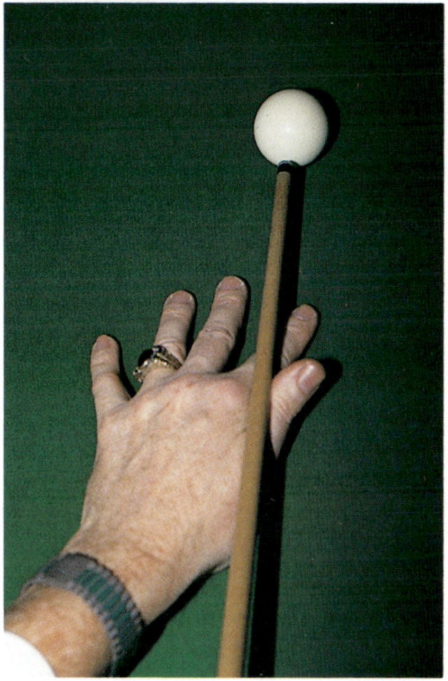

▲ *Place the bridge hand so that the cue will rest on it, with the tip almost touching and able to strike the cue ball*

Main photograph: *a comfortable stance, from the side.* Inset: *adjust the feet and legs until the stance is comfortable and steady* ▶

Striking the cue ball

Before attempting shots at an object ball, practise with the cue ball only. Place the ball in the 'D' at the head of the table and take up your stance comfortably. Sight along the cue, through the cue ball, to a position on the bottom cushion, exactly opposite the cue ball, until you are confident that you are moving the cue in a true line towards the centre of the cue ball and the target spot on the bottom cushion.

When you are satisfied, allow the cue to travel forwards to strike the cue ball. Do not strike too hard. Try to judge the force of your stroke so that the cue ball will return from the bottom cushion and come to rest at the tip of your waiting cue.

This is an excellent practice stroke and it will pay enormous dividends to the player who can master it. Control of the cue ball, both before and after striking the target, must be regarded as the most important of the many skills required to make a good player. This skill is the one which ensures that you consistently win. Therefore, for the beginner and the competent player, no time is ever wasted that is spent practising the exact control of the cue ball.

Cushions

Many beginners have difficulty, initially, working out the angles of shots played against the cushion. It may help to think of it in the following manner. If a tennis ball is dropped on to a flat surface, it will rebound in a straight line. However, should it be thrown at a slight angle it will bounce away at an angle equal to that at which it approached the ground. A pool ball reacts in exactly the same manner when striking the cushion of the table (*see* fig. 2). Unless 'side' has been put on to the ball, angles A and B will always be equal. The ability to 'play all the angles' is essential and fine judgement is called for.

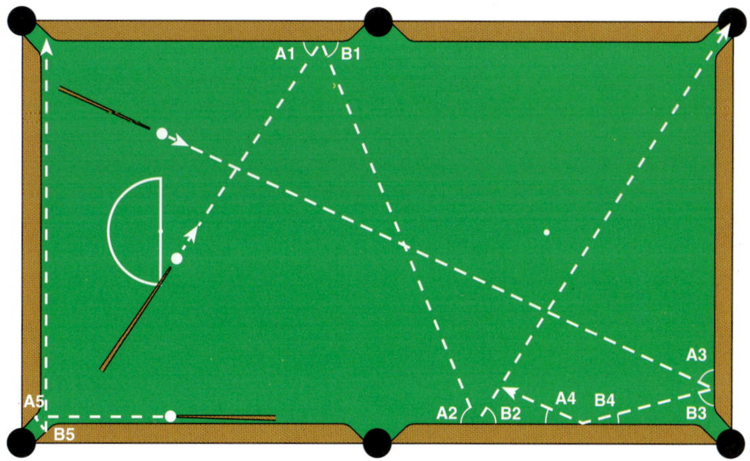

▲ *Fig. 2 Practising the angles: angles of shots played full ball against the cushion*

Check and side

The way you strike the cue ball will determine its action when it contacts an object ball or cushion.

By striking the cue ball below the centre line you can increase the degree of 'check' on its progress when it strikes an object ball. The lower the strike, the greater the check, until, if hit at its lowest point, the cue ball will hit the object ball and 'screw back', or return along the cue-line. The ability to do this is invaluable when you are attempting to pot a straight ball into the pocket without following it in with the cue ball, which would make a foul stroke ('in off').

If the cue ball is struck above the centre line, the degree of check is decreased on impact and it will increasingly tend to 'follow through' according to how high it has been struck.

The cue ball can also be steered after it strikes an object ball. If it is struck to the left of the centre it will run to the left, and if struck to the right of centre it will run to the right. This is referred to as putting 'side' on the cue ball and is sometimes useful to change the angle of the cue ball as it returns from the cushion.

These strikes are combined to produce right-hand check or follow-through, and left-hand check or follow-through. Since the degree to which all these things are varied can vastly change the action of the cue ball, it will be seen that the advice to practise is important. Only experimentation will determine what you personally can achieve.

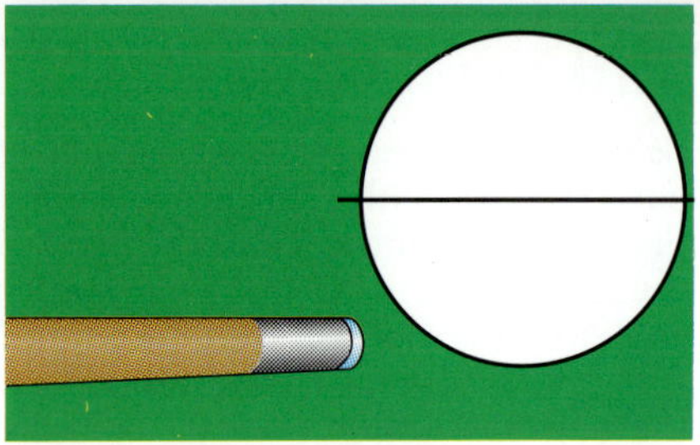

▲▼ *Fig. 3 To apply check, strike the cue ball* below *the centre line*

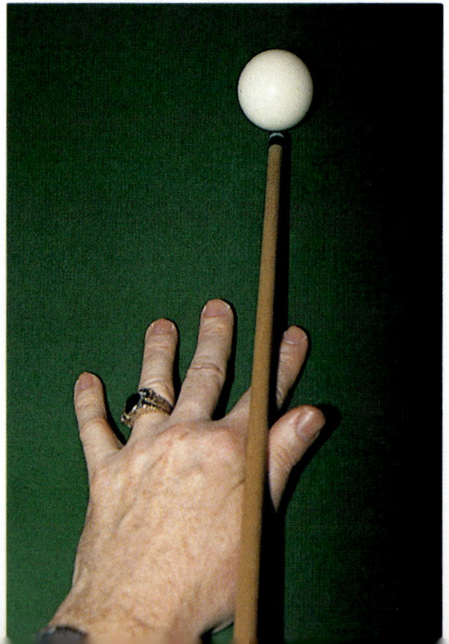

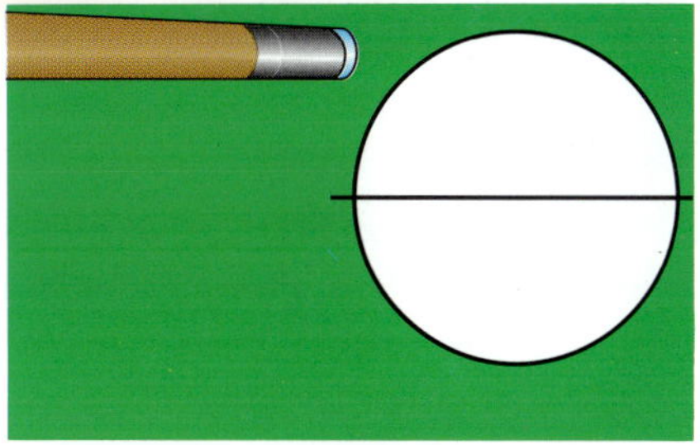

▲▼ *Fig. 4 To apply follow through, strike the cue ball* above *the centre line*

▲▼ *Fig. 5 To apply left-hand side, strike the cue ball to the* left *of the centre line*

▲▼ *Fig. 6 To apply right-hand side, strike the cue ball to the* right *of the centre line*

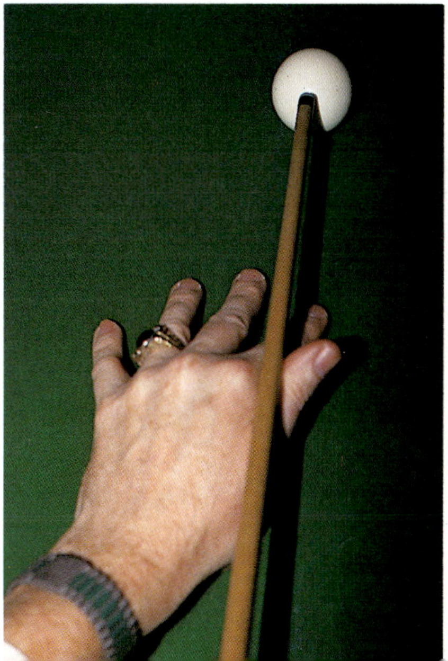

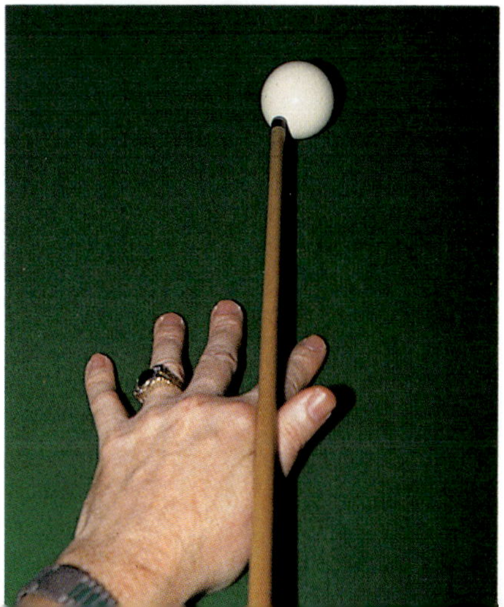

▲ *Fig. 7 Swerve: spin is applied to the cue ball to project it around the obstructing ball*

◀ *Applying swerve to the cue ball is an advanced technique, not strictly for the beginner*

Potting

Direction

To pot an object ball, it is important to ensure that the cue ball strikes it at the correct point. For a straight shot, this should be the centre, but when cutting the ball into a pocket to the left of the line from cue ball to object ball, the object ball should be struck on the right, and on the opposite side for a pocket to the right.

Momentum

When the cue ball strikes an object ball, it imparts momentum to it. The nearer to the centre of the object ball that the cue ball strikes, the greater the momentum it will gain and the less acute the angle of travel will be. Conversely, the nearer the outside the object ball is struck by the cue ball, the less momentum is transferred and the wider the angle of travel.

Thus, an object ball struck full face will travel at almost the same speed as the striking cue ball, while an object ball struck on the extreme edge will gain very little momentum. It is apparent, then, that the more accurately the object ball is required to be struck, the more delicate is the judgement needed in assessing the force required. Many players can be seen blazing away with unnecessary force, incurring penalties which with practice and forethought could have been avoided.

Cue-ball position

The cue ball bounces from the object ball in a very similar manner to that in which it bounces from the cushion, apart from the momentum it loses. Always keep in mind the direction the cue ball will take after striking the object ball. Ensure that it goes where you want it, so that it works to your advantage, not your opponent's. Remember: *control that cue ball.*

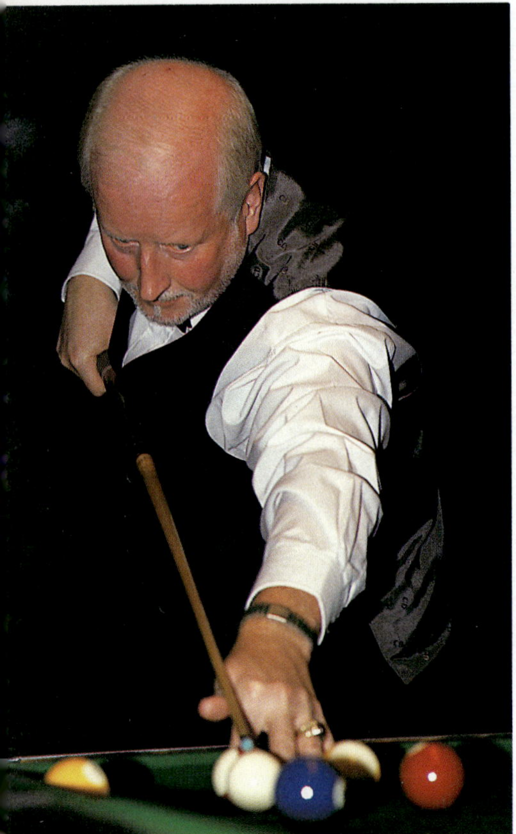

Playing the game

Note on the rules

The rules, which can be found on pages 40–3, are quite brief and were carefully written by BAPTO in 1975. Modifications to the rules have been made since then with the aim of maintaining the maximum fairness to participants and to eradicate those rules which have been abused by unscrupulous players. There is frequently discussion among players about exactly what is meant by particular rules, and about points not mentioned. The explanation of the game which follows is an attempt to help with some of these problems, but our most urgent advice is that where there is discussion and a lack of authoritative knowledge, the players or teams should agree on what is fair before play commences.

It is important in any competition or league to rule that if a match is played or continued after a dispute, any irregularity will be deemed to have been condoned, and the result will stand by the referee's decision with no possibility of appeal.

Terminology

- **Shot** – striking the cue ball once.
- **Visit** – one turn at the table comprising one or a series of shots.
- **Break** – first shot of the game or first shot of a re-started game.

Racking

The first step in the game is to place the balls on the table in the form of a solid triangle, using the rack provided. The black ball is placed on the 8-ball spot marked on the table.

The triangle fans out towards the bottom cushion with the head (single) ball facing the 'D', and with balls of different combination at the corners. The 8-ball is racked in the centre of the third row and placed on the spot which is at the intersection of the centre and corner pockets. The remainder of the balls are placed as depicted in the photographs on this page.

▲ *Correctly racked balls* ▲

Starting the game

Order of play is decided by tossing a coin. The winner of the toss can choose to make the first shot himself, or ask his opponent to do so.

The opening player places the cue ball at any point on or within the 'D', and plays it at the triangle of object balls. He must either pocket a ball or drive at least two balls to hit the cushion. If he does neither, a foul break has occurred, the balls are re-racked and the opposing player re-starts the game with two visits: thus the offending player loses a turn at the table.

If a player pockets a ball from the break, that ball denotes the player's numerical (or colour) group. If a player pockets one ball from each numerical group on the break, he can nominate his choice and continue to play. The unnominated ball remains pocketed, as do all balls throughout the game, however pocketed, except the cue ball.

The break ▶

If no balls are pocketed from the break, the oncoming player must nominate his choice and continue to play on his nominated group. Any illegally pocketed ball is ignored in determining which group the players are on.

If a foul shot is committed at the break and one or more object balls pocketed, those balls are ignored in determining the groups to be played, and the next player plays at any ball on the table (except the 8-ball); the first to be pocketed denotes his group. This rule applies to the break (first) shot only, not to any subsequent shots.

If a player pockets the 8-ball from the break, the game shall be re-started by the same player. This applies only on the break, not on any subsequent shots.

When a player legally pockets a ball or balls, he will continue by playing another shot. This carries on until he either fails to pocket one of his group of object balls or commits a foul.

Combination shots (i.e. when the cue ball hits an object ball which then hits another object ball) are allowed, provided the player hits one of his own object balls first. Following a foul, a player may, on his first shot only, hit any ball on the table (*see* Rule 6).

Snooker

A player is snookered when he does not have a 'full ball shot' at any of his balls. This means that, looking in a straight line from behind the cue ball to the object ball in question, he cannot see the whole circumference of his ball, i.e. the centre of the object ball cannot be struck by the centre of the cue ball. It does not matter whether one of the sides can be played and, in this respect, pool differs from the game of snooker.

A snookered ball can be played off a cushion.

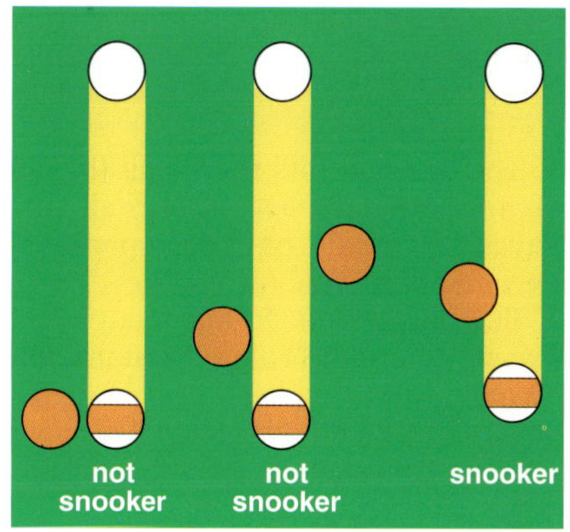

Fig. 8 Identifying a snooker ▶

Fouls

When a foul is committed, the oncoming player is awarded an extra shot. It is a foul when any of the following occurs.

- The white cue ball is pocketed. This is known as 'in off'. If this occurs, the cue ball is replaced at any position on or within the 'D'.
- The cue ball strikes the opponent's ball before the player's own ball or balls.
- The player fails to hit any ball with the cue ball.
- The cue ball jumps over any part of any ball by accident or design before hitting any ball at all. This is known as a 'jump shot'.
- The cue ball hits the 8-ball (black) on the first impact before all the player's own balls have been pocketed (except where Rule 6(b) applies).
- The player pots an opponent's ball (except where the rule on penalty following any foul applies – *see* below). If a player pots the 8-ball before all his own balls are pocketed, he loses the game.
- A ball goes off the table. If it is any object ball, it should be placed on the 8-ball spot or as near as possible to the 8-ball spot in a direct line between the head spot and the centre of the 'D'. A ball is deemed to be off the table if it comes to rest anywhere other than on the bed of the table.
- A player's clothing or body touches any ball. Even if the ball does not move, a foul should be called.
- A player does not have at least one foot on the floor.
- A player strikes with the cue any ball other than the cue ball.
- A player plays out of turn.
- A player plays before all balls have come to rest.
- A player plays before the ball or balls have been re-spotted (i.e. replaced in the appropriate places).
- A player interferes with the movement of the ball with body, clothing or cue.
- A player strikes the cue ball with the cue more than once.
- A player plays a push shot, whereby the cue stays in contact as the cue ball rolls.

▲ *A foul is committed if the cue ball strikes an opponent's ball before the player's own ball. In this case, the player playing the spotted balls cannot legally play a shot to strike his last remaining ball, the 6-ball: the balls shall be re-racked and the game restarted by this player*

▲ *A foul is committed if the cue ball jumps over any part of any ball*

▲ *A foul is committed if a player does not have at least one foot on the floor*

▲ *A foul is committed if a player strikes with the cue any ball other than the cue ball*

Penalty for a foul

The penalty for a foul is for a player to concede one extra shot to his opponent. Formerly a player lost his next visit to the table; however, since the introduction of the cue ball in-hand whereby the offended player is permitted to move the cue ball to anywhere within the 'D', that penalty has been considered too severe. Therefore, the oncoming player has one free shot, irrespective of whether an object ball is potted or not, before commencing his due turn or visit to the table.

It should be noted that it is the offended player's duty to claim his full entitlement. If he allows his opponent to play prior to his full entitlement, he cannot claim afterwards any part of his missed entitlement. On the other hand, the opponent has played out of turn and in so doing has committed a foul.

A referee in this situation is not bound to prompt either player unless asked for advice, and just administers the rules.

Following any foul, the oncoming player, for the first shot of his first visit only, is free to play at any ball without nomination and without penalty, including his opponent's ball and the 8-ball (black), whether or not he is snookered. All balls potted directly or by combination are considered legally potted (except the 8-ball, which would lose him the game) and entitle him to an additional shot(s) as described in Rule 4(h).

After any foul stroke, the offended player may play the ball from where it lies or from any position within the 'D'. Moving the ball in this way does not count as a shot or visit.

Winning the game

When a player has potted all seven of his object balls, he finishes and wins the game by potting the 8-ball. It is not necessary to nominate the pocket in which the black (or any other ball) is potted; therefore a fluke pot is still sufficient to win the game.

A player potting the 8-ball and any other ball on the same stroke will lose the game except following a foul when only the 8-ball and one or more ball(s) of his opponent's group are left, in which case he may legally pot the 8-ball and others in any order.

Drawn game

Should any situation arise whereby a legal shot cannot be played, the game shall be re-started whether the situation has arisen by accident or design.

Stalemate

In any sort of pool competition a referee should be appointed. If it seems that both players intend to play a continuous sequence of non-potting safe shots, the referee may intervene and give notice of his intention to re-start the game if the position remains in stalemate after the next visit to the table by both players.

Strategy

Pool differs substantially from snooker and billiards in playing strategy, as many an old hand at snooker has discovered with embarrassment. In snooker and billiards, few if any balls are denied to a player provided he has followed the correct sequence. In pool, however, seven balls plus the black may not be played or potted, from almost the commencement of the game, without incurring penalties.

Thus, a player can 'cover' the pockets of the table. By placing object balls of his own group in a position near a pocket, he can effectively deny the use of that pocket to his opponent. The accomplished player will often be seen to take a more difficult shot, rather than sink a ball sitting over a pocket. This does not mean that it has escaped his notice, but that the 'sitter' is almost certainly making it difficult for his opponent to progress.

This pool strategy also explains why a good player does not always sink the ball played towards a pocket. Frequently the ball is of more value left on the table until he is able to clean up by potting all his object balls followed by the black 8-ball.

You must always bear in mind that your objective is not only to pot your own balls, but also to ensure that you prevent your opponent potting his. By obstructing his play with your own object balls and placing the cue ball in positions to cause him the greatest difficulty, you will do much to improve your own chances of success. It must be remembered, however, that you cannot win a game *without* potting balls, and playing in an over-cautious manner can often benefit your opponent more than yourself.

There is one final word of advice for all players – relax. Pool is not a game that can be played well in an excitable frame of mind. You will never be likely to win any game of importance by a hurried and ill-considered approach. Concentrate on what you wish to achieve and put other thoughts out of your head. Think about how you will play to win. By doing this you will give yourself that extra 'edge' that wins matches.

▲ *Players often choose to cover pockets in the early stages in anticipation of an opportunity later in the game to clear their balls in one or two visits to the table.* See also *Rule 4(j) on page 41*

◀ *You cannot win a game without potting balls!*

Competition organisation

The injection of challenge and incentive is as essential to pool as to most successful sports. League and knockout competitions will keep the adrenalin surging over a sustained period, and friendly matches are a marvellous way of highlighting the social benefits to be enjoyed from local rivalries.

Before we get down to the mechanics of organising competitions, it is important to consider carefully the interests of everyone concerned, namely the landlord of the premises (who may be brewery, proprietor or licensee), the pool players and the non-pool-playing users of the premises.

The landlord will be at pains to increase his business by keeping his pool players happy without alienating those of his customers who do not play the game and who may resent an invasion of their privacy by players and spectators from another place. His is a very difficult job. In the circumstances,

the landlord should always be involved in the decisions of his players to take part in a competition.

Leagues

The first step is to establish the degree of interest. This will usually take the form of a letter of invitation containing outline proposals, including such matters as:

- area in which the league is to operate
- over what period the season should run
- match nights and starting times
- rules for 8-ball pool
- constitution, i.e. conditions to supplement 8-ball rules (*see* pages 40–3)
- sponsorships or other prizes
- number of teams per location
- number of players/registrations (e.g. six players registered to ensure there is always a team of four available, and 12 registered for a team of eight)
- number of teams per league
- pool table specifications
- registration fees
- committees
- referees.

Broadly speaking, this procedure would apply for area knock-out competitions, but for individual house competitions most of the formalities may be dispensed with.

Assuming that there is sufficient response – and the organisers have told everyone concerned of their intentions – the next step is to decide on the type and amount of advertising and other supporting literature required to launch the competition. Unless one is lucky enough to find a sponsor to foot the bill, this can prove a most costly item. The alternative is to use one's own resources as much as possible, but it is usually a false economy to produce 'cheap and nasty' visuals, particularly posters.

The following items are essential.

Posters

An eye-catching poster should be produced to announce the competition, the prizes and how to enter.

Match posters are also useful in that they may well increase business on the night, quite apart from their information value.

Registration forms

These can be typed and copied if resources do not run to the cost of producing printed team or individual cards, ideally with photographs of players. Registration cards should be prepared in duplicate, one copy to be kept by the organisers and the other stamped and returned to the team for production at matches.

The forms should be distributed with posters, and authenticated before the first matches are due to be played. Registration is often subject to abuse and competition organisers would be well advised to ensure that only registered players represent a particular team. It should be possible to establish a reasonably accurate system of cross-checking names and signatures on result cards with those on the organiser's copy of registration forms.

REGISTRATION CARD

TEAM NAME ______________________________ **Tel.** __________

& ADDRESS ______________________________ __________

	Name	Signature		Name	Signature
1			7		
2			8		
3			9		
4			10		
5			11		
6			12		

Name and Signature of Landlord ______________________________ DATE __________

▲ *Fig. 9 A registration card*

RESULT CARD

Home Team .... Away Team..

	Home Name	Home Signature	Away Name	Away Signature
1				
2				
3				
4				
5				
6				
7				
8				
9				

Date________ Comp't'n/Div__________ Home Score________ Away Score________

Home ____________________ Away Captain ____________________

▲ *Fig. 10 A result card*

Results sheets

These, too, may be produced locally, but a pre-paid postcard is likely to ensure a better response to the need for speedy reporting of match results.

Fixture lists

There may be two separate types of fixture list. It is important to publish one list for the full season, and if this can be supplemented by monthly fixture lists, so much the better.

Each team should be scheduled to play each other team in the league once away and once at home each season. The compilation of fixture lists can be a mathematician's nightmare, particularly if there are houses with two teams in divisions with different numbers of teams. It is necessary to always ensure that houses with two teams avoid a clash of home venue. It is somewhat easier to achieve this when each division in an organised league accommodates the same number of teams.

It is both necessary and desirable to pre-plan dates for all competitions being organised, and you will see in the following example that a clear date has been reserved for knock-out competitions at the stage where all teams are involved. You will also note that certain numbers in the fixture formula are 'paired', e.g. numbers 2 and 7 are never 'at home' on the same day, so these pairings are used for locations with two teams but only one pool table.

It is always desirable to draw attention to anything out of the ordinary, hence the note below advising teams in one division that there are some fixtures scheduled for an alternative day to the rest of the fixtures.

Fixtures for the Joe Bloggs Bloggsville & District League. The following fixtures apply to all divisions except "D" division

Oct3	**Oct10**	**Oct17**	**Oct24**	**Oct31**	**Nov7**	**Nov14**	**Nov21**	**Nov28**	**Dec5**	**Dec12**
2v1	1v3	4v1	1v5	Team KO		6v1	1v7	8v1	1v9	10v1
3v9	10v2	3v2	2v4	7 Man		5v2	2v6	7v2	2v8	9v2
4v8	9v4	5v9	10v3	Home & Away		4v3	3v5	6v3	3v7	8v3
5v7	8v5	6v8	9v6	Aggregate		7v9	10v4	5v4	4v6	7v4
6v10	7v6	7v10	8v7	will count		8v10	9v8	9v10	10v5	6v5
Jan9	**Jan16**	**Jan23**	**Jan30**			**Feb20**	**Feb27**	**Mar6**	**Mar13**	**Mar23**

Singles first round will be on December 19; 3-team KO Feb 6 & 13.

The following fixtures apply to "D" division. Note the four Wednesday matches.

Oct3	**Oct10**	**Oct17**	**Oct24**	**Wed Nov2**	**Wed Nov9**	**Nov14**	**Nov21**	**Nov28**	**Dec5**	**Dec12**
2v1	1v3	4v1	1v5	1v11	12v1	6v1	1v7	8v1	1v9	10v1
3v11	12v2	3v2	2v4	2v10	11v2	5v2	2v6	7v2	2v8	9v2
4v10	11v4	5v11	12v3	3v9	10v3	4v3	3v5	6v3	3v7	8v3
5v9	10v5	6v10	11v6	4v8	9v4	7v11	12v4	5v4	4v6	7v4
6v8	9v6	7v9	10v7	5v7	8v5	8v10	11v8	9v11	12v5	6v5
7v12	8v7	8v12	9v8	6v12	7v6	9v12	10v9	10v12	11v10	11v12
Jan9	**Jan16**	**Jan23**	**Jan30**	**Feb1**	**Feb15**	**Feb20**	**Feb27**	**Mar6**	**Mar13**	**Mar20**

continued overleaf

"A" Division	"B" Division	"C" Division
(1) Talbot "C"	(1) Talbot "A"	(1) Black Bull "B"
(2) Brunshaw "B"	(2) Bridge "A"	(2) Gen. Havelock "A"
(3) Station (Nelson)	(3) Dragoon "B"	(3) Griffin "A"
(4) Corporation "A"	(4) Wellington	(4) Woodman "A"
(5) Gannow Wharf "A"	(5) Rose & Crown	(5) Old Duke
(6) Black Bull "A"	(6) Talbot "B"	(6) Rifle Vols "B"
(7) Brunshaw "A"	(7) Briercliffe W.M.C.	(7) Gen. Havelock "B"
(8) Dragoon "A"	(8) Bay Horse	(8) Town Mouse "A"
(9) Corporation "C"	(9) Waggoners "A"	(9) Corporation "B"
(10) Frames	(10) Dugdale	(10) Mitre
"D" Division	"E" Division	"F" Division
(1) Adelphi	(1) Fighting Cocks "B"	(1) Cattle Market
(2) Alma	(2) Carlton W.M.C.	(2) Bridge "C"
(3) Borough	(3) Griffin "B"	(3) Town Mouse "B"
(4) Brickmakers "A"	(4) Royal Butterfly	(4) Waggoners "B"
(5) Marsden Cross	(5) Concert Artists "A"	(5) Louie's "B"
(6) Old Bridge	(6) Nelson	(6) Talbot "D"
(7) Fighting Cocks "A"	(7) Coach & Horses	(7) Rose & Thistle
(8) Bridge "B"	(8) Feathers	(8) Dragoon "C"
(9) Oxford	(9) Gordon Lennox	(9) Woodman "B"
(10) Brickmakers "B"	(10) Gannow Wharf "B"	(10) Concert Artists "B"
(11) Louie's "A"		
(12) Rifle Vols "A"		

Rules and constitution

The benefits of playing to a standard set of rules will be immediately apparent and the official BAPTO rules appear on pages 40–3. A rules chart should be prominently displayed wherever pool is played.

In addition to the basic rules for 8-ball pool, there will be conditions and procedures which are appropriate to that particular competition. These should be prominently displayed or readily available on match nights.

A little extra polish to the proceedings will result if players and officials can be provided with pocket-sized cards containing the rules, the constitution and notes for the guidance of referees.

Timetable

So that events and requirements may be properly planned, organisers may find it useful to produce something along the lines of the specimen 'critical path analysis' illustrated on this page. It will be seen that not all the literature is required at once and that more than one activity can be planned to take place simultaneously.

Having placed the orders for the paperwork, the organisers must decide how the league is to be run, i.e. by themselves, a representative committee, or the sponsors, and arrange a meeting as soon as possible. Whichever method is adopted, it will be necessary to apportion responsibilities and establish procedures for dealing with disputes, etc. Large committees tend to become too unwieldy to be effective and should be avoided at all costs.

If the suggestion to keep a timetable of events has been followed, the organisers should be in a position to issue the balance of the competition kit about two weeks before the first matches are due to be played. This kit should comprise the following items:

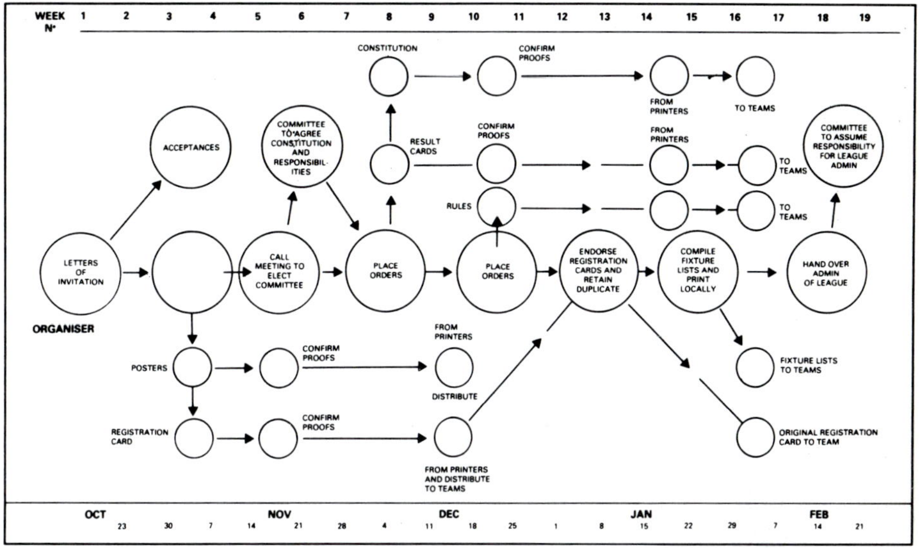

▲ *Fig. 11 Example of a critical path analysis for pool*

- endorsed registration
- sufficient result cards for half a season
- rules card
- constitution
- match posters and individual pocket cards, if available.

Midway through the competition, posters and rule cards should be replaced by fresh material and the second batch of result cards. A small reserve of all supporting literature and promotional material should be retained for replacements.

Publicity

Try to get as much local press coverage as possible. At the very least, most local papers will be happy to publish league results and tables on a regular basis.

When it comes to organising competitions, the drones will far outnumber the workers, and there will be times when you wonder why you ever bothered. However, provided that your planning is good and your administration sound, the criticisms you hear will be those of the bad losers – and they don't count.

Tournaments

A well-run tournament will go a long way towards achieving wholesome competition as opposed to confrontation, and the players themselves will usually lift their game to fit the occasion.

Tournaments may be team or individual affairs and usually concern the winners of some earlier rounds or minor competitions. Either way, it is fundamental that the number of contestants can be handled within available resources of finance, equipment, manpower, time and space.

Planning

In considering a budget for the event, it is probably better that fewer people compete for bigger prizes than the reverse, and the ability to advertise the tournament on the basis of worthwhile awards is likely to attract more entrants in the initial stages of the competition. Money will need to be apportioned for hire of venue, audio, lighting and other equipment, officials, promotional literature and so on.

Apart from special equipment, the pool tables to be used should be chosen with care so that, as far as possible, no player can be seen to enjoy an advantage over another.

The time available for the tournament should be calculated along with the number of tables required. In this connection, there is a simple and useful formula for all knock-out competitions: the number of *matches* to be played is always one less than the number of competitors. For example, four competitors: two semi-finals, plus one final = three games; 119 competitors involves 55 preliminary matches and nine byes to reduce to 64 entrants; 32 first round matches followed in subsequent rounds by 16, eight, four and two culminating in one final match to total 118.

The maximum number of *games* required is then calculated on the basis of whatever criteria constitute a match, e.g. one game only, best of three, etc. Singles will normally take not more than 15 minutes, and 20 minutes should usually be sufficient for doubles. However, one can always stipulate a time limit for games if necessary.

With this kind of information at hand, it is not too difficult to calculate how many tables or how much time is needed to complete a particular programme. Overcrowding of any kind must be avoided, as jostling among players or spectators is likely to cause aggravation and chaos.

In allocating order for play, the organisers would do well to ensure that all pool tables are fully utilised, even if it means having more than one stage or competition running simultaneously. In the interests of fair play, care should be taken to see that winning players are not allocated the same table throughout the competition.

Types of tournament

Tournaments can take many forms.

- Straight run knock-out competitions, reducing from a given number of contestants to an outright winner on an eliminator basis; simple and easy to run.
- Double elimination knock-out competitions where first time losers have an opportunity to stay in the competition by being drawn against other losers; this can be complicated and time-consuming.
- Grouping of contestants as in the soccer World Cup, followed by a knock-out competition between group winners; popular with players, as they stay in the competition that much longer.

Rules for success

Whatever method you choose, keep everyone informed of what is going on at every stage of the tournament. Good visual aids will amply repay the effort of producing them.

Possibly the best investment of all lies in the employment of officials. Professional referees have presence and ability and command respect from players and spectators alike. Clear and concise announcements on a good public address system assist the smooth flow of the competition through all its stages. Efficient and courteous service at the bar and food counters removes a possible source of irritation, and capable door attendants can ensure that gate-crashers are refused admission.

Remember the following golden rules and you will be well on the way to organising a successful pool tournament.

- Make sure money and prizes are available as advertised.
- Do not try to achieve too much in the time available.
- Select the best possible premises in terms of space.
- Use only first-class tables and ancilliary equipment.
- Employ efficient and courteous manpower in all departments.
- Get your sums right.
- Keep everyone informed of what is happening.
- Avoid overcrowding.

Notes for referees

(1) It is important that the referee understands the game rules and he must be assured that the players also have read and understood the same rules.

(2) The referee must also have read and understood the rules governing the procedure of that competition or league and must be assured that the players have also read and understood the same rules.

(3) The referee shall determine the conduct for the match in progress and is empowered to abandon, postpone or disqualify.

Abandonment means a NIL result for both parties. Postponement allows a second chance to establish a result and in certain circumstances can be done immediately by re-starting a game. Disqualification of one or other of the parties gives the game to the other.

(4) Careful thought must be given before deciding on a course of drastic action as in note (3). It is advisable to suspend play and then talk to the two players or two captains before making a final decision. If ever in doubt of a decision, the referee should suspend play immediately, obtain what facts he can, then make his decision.

(5) It is advisable to draw the two captains aside before the game starts and briefly run over certain points which are often not widely understood, and make quite clear what interpretation the referee will make, for example:

(a) following a foul, the oncoming (innocent) player is granted a free shot in which he may play the ball from where it lies or from within the 'D', and may play any ball, but must not pot the black. Following this free single shot, the player's visit to the table commences
(b) the cue ball may be played in any direction from within the 'D', which is also described as 'cue ball in hand'
(c) player in control rule – vibration pot (*see* note (16) below)
(d) the referee should clarify what happens if a player is unable or unwilling to complete the game.

(6) Before the beginning of the game the referee must ensure that the balls are correctly racked, with the 8-ball (black) in the centre of the third row on the spot at the intersection of the centre and bottom pockets, the others alternating high and low wherever possible. This method of racking the balls has proven to produce the fairest spread of object balls following the break.

(7) The referee should ensure that both captains understand what situations may result in the loss of a game:

(a) illegal potting of the 8-ball (Rules 7(a), (b) and (c))
(b) cue or any object ball in off the 8-ball when the 8-ball is legally potted.

(8) If a player deliberately alters the course of a ball or obstructs a pocket opening, a foul shall be awarded.

(9) If anyone other than the two players interferes with the playing of the game, then the referee at that time can choose the option of either having the balls replaced in their original positions and the shot replayed, or restarting the game.

(10) In the event of a player or players being considered incapable of offering fair and just competition because of either drink or drugs, the referee should be prepared to warn initially. If competition is unrealistic, play should be suspended, but the referee should try to arrive at an amicable solution before making his final decision.

(11) Dependent on the rules of that particular competition or league, a substitute may be allowed, providing that the player satisfies registration conditions.

(12) If a player is deliberately coached by any other player or spectator, then the referee, at his discretion, will warn that further occurrences will cause the game to be abandoned, or awarded at his discretion.

(13) The referee shall call all fouls and penalties and will make it clear to the players when they have to cease playing.

(14) In the event of a player being about to play an obvious foul stroke the referee shall not warn him before the stroke is taken (*see* note (17)).

(15) The referee shall not proffer any advice nor warn a player before a stroke. He may give a ruling if approached by a player before taking his shot.

(16) In the event of a ball being accidentally vibrated into a pocket then the player in control rule shall apply. A player is deemed to be 'in control' from the time that any part of him, including clothing and cue, touches the table prior to his shot, through his visit and until such time as his opponent does likewise prior to his shot.

(17) The referee shall ensure that both players are clear on which group of object balls they are playing for. This is particularly important where a player has potted one or more of either set and is taking a choice.

(18) The referee should take particular care when a player is playing away from a touching ball or aiming a shot which could produce a foul shot by the player not striking his own set of object balls first.

(19) The referee should take particular care when a player is making a high bridge over his own or opponent's balls, and take particular note of the cuff of the sleeve if a coat is being worn by the player.

(20) To miscue a ball shall not be a foul in itself. A foul may only be called on the result of the stroke.

(21) The referee may not wager or accept any remuneration on the result of a game.

(22) The referee shall ensure that the score card is properly marked and signed by officials according to the rules of the league or competition in which they are entered.

Rules of 8-ball pool

(1) The game

The game shall be known as 8-ball pool and referred to in these rules as 'the game'. It is intended that players and teams should play 8-ball pool in the true spirit of the game and in a sportsmanlike manner. It should be clearly understood that the referee is the sole judge of what is fair and unfair play. The referee will take whatever action is necessary to ensure that these rules are observed.

(2) Requirements of the game

The game is played on a rectangle six-pocket table with 15 balls, plus a cue ball. Balls comprise two groups, represented by two different coloured balls plus the 8-ball which is black.

Alternatively, numerical balls may be used, numbered 1–7 which are plain coloured balls, 9–15 which are striped coloured balls.

Balls in two groups are known as object balls.

(3) Object of the game

The player or team pocketing their group of object balls first in any order and then legally pocketing the 8-ball (black), wins the game.

(4) Commencement of the game (or re-start)

(a) The balls are racked as illustrated in the photographs on page 21 with the 8-ball (black) on the 8-ball spot which is at the intersection of the centre and corner pockets.

(b) Order of play is determined by the flip of a coin. The winner of the flip has the option of breaking or requesting his opponent to do so.

(c) The opening player plays at the triangle of object balls by striking the cue ball from any position on or within the 'D'. He must pocket a ball or cause at least two object balls to hit a cushion. Failure to do so is a foul break and will result in the balls being re-racked. The opposing player re-starts the game with one break shot followed by one visit.

(d) On the break, if a player legally pockets an object ball, then that denotes his group, unless he pockets balls from each group, when he must nominate his choice before continuing to play.

(e) If no ball is pocketed from a legal break, then the oncoming player must clearly nominate his choice of group of object balls before play continues.

(f) If a foul is committed on the break other than as in 4(g), any balls pocketed are ignored in determining groups.

(g) If the player pockets the 8-ball (black) from the break, the game shall be re-started by the same player. No penalty will be incurred. The balls to be re-racked. This applies even if other balls, including the cue ball, are pocketed as well.

(h) If a ball or balls are legally pocketed, this entitles the player to one additional shot and this continues until the player either:

(i) fails to pocket one of his set of allocated balls, or

(ii) commits a foul, at any time.

(i) Combination shots are allowed provided that the player hits one of his own group of balls first (unless Rule 6(b) applies).

(j) A player may legally pocket one or more of his opponent's object ball/s providing the cue ball strikes one of his own group first and providing one or more of his own group are pocketed on the same shot.

(5) Fouls

(a) In off (cue ball pocketed).

(b) Hitting opponent's balls before his own ball or balls, except when Rule 6(b) applies.

(c) Failing to hit any ball with the cue ball.

(d) Jump shots – defined as when the cue ball jumps over any part of any ball before making contact with any object ball.

(e) If a player hits the 8-ball (black) with the cue ball on the first impact before all his own balls have been potted, except when Rule 6(b) applies.

(f) Potting any opponent's balls except when Rule 4(j) or 6(b) applies.

(g) Ball off the table.

(i) Any object ball or the 8-ball (black) shall be returned to the 8-ball spot (*see* 4(a)) or as near as possible to that spot without touching any other ball, in a direct line between the spot and the centre of the 'D'.

(ii) If the cue ball, the ball to be played from any position on or within the 'D'. A ball shall be deemed to be 'off the table' if it comes to rest other than on the bed of the table.

(h) If a player's clothing or body should touch any ball.

(i) Player not having at least one foot on the floor.

(j) Playing or touching with the cue any ball other than the cue ball.

(k) Playing out of turn.

(l) Playing before balls have come to rest.

(m) Playing before the ball or balls have been re-spotted.

(n) Striking the cue ball with any part of the cue other than the tip.

(o) Striking the cue ball with the cue more than once.

(p) Failing to clearly nominate when Rule 4(d) or 4(f) applies.

(q) Foul break (*see* 4(c)).

(r) Push stroke (*see* 8(a)).

(s) Moving an object ball or the 8-ball (black) when playing away from a touching ball.

(6) Penalty following any foul

(a) Following any foul described under Rule 5, the oncoming player may play the cue ball from where it lies or from the 'D' (as in Rule 8(b)) and proceed as 6(b). Moving the cue ball to the 'D' does not constitute a shot or visit.

(b) Following a foul, the oncoming player is entitled to one free shot with which he may, without nomination, play the cue ball directly on to any ball, including opponent's object balls and the 8-ball (black). However, he may not pocket the 8-ball (black) which would mean loss of the game, unless the player has already pocketed all of his own group of object balls and only needs to pocket the 8-ball (black) to win the game.

(c) Following the single free shot described in 6(a) the player will commence his normal visit.

(7) Loss of game

(a) If a player pockets the 8-ball (black) before he pockets all balls in his own group, except as allowed under Rule 4(g), he loses the game.

(b) A player going in off the 8-ball (black) when the 8-ball (black) is potted, loses the game.

(c) A player who clearly fails to make any attempt to play a ball of his own group will lose the game.

(d) If a player seeks to gain advantage by deliberately touching a moving ball or retrieving a ball dropping into the pocket he shall lose the game.

(8) General

(a) **Push stroke** – defined as when the tip of the cue remains in contact with the cue ball once it has commenced its forward motion.

(b) **Cue ball in hand** – when a player has the cue ball in hand he plays from any position on or within the 'D' and in any direction.

(c) **Player in control** – a player is said to be in control of the table from the time that his body, cue or clothing touches the table prior to his shot, through his visit and up until his opponent does likewise prior to his visit. Any balls which fall into the pockets during this period (including 8-ball (black)), he is said to have potted and he is liable to any penalties or benefits normally awarded to him for the potting of that ball or balls as are accorded to him in the rules of the game (Rule 5(c) applies).

(d) The game is completed when the 8-ball (black) is potted in any pocket and all the remaining balls including the cue ball have come to rest, except where Rule 4(g) applies.

(e) **Touching ball** – a player must play away from a touching ball which must not move (*see* 5(s)). If the touching ball is one of the player's own group, he is deemed to have played that ball. If the touching ball is not one of his own group, the cue ball must strike one of his own group. When 6(b) applies a player must play away from a touching ball and is deemed to have played that ball.

(9) Stalemate

Should any situation arise whereby a legal shot cannot be played, then the game shall be re-started by the same player whether this situation is arrived at by accident or design. If in the opinion of the referee neither player is allowing the game to progress or a stalemate situation has arisen, then the game shall be re-started by the same player.

Guidance

(a) The term 'shot' means striking the cue ball once.

(b) The term 'visit' refers to one term at the table comprising one of a series of shots.

(c) The term 'break' refers to the first shot of the game or the first shot of a game being re-started.

(d) Coaching is deemed to be unsportsmanlike (*see* Rule 1).

(e) A referee may, if requested, advise on rules of the game.

Reproduced by kind permission of the United Kingdom Pool Federation.

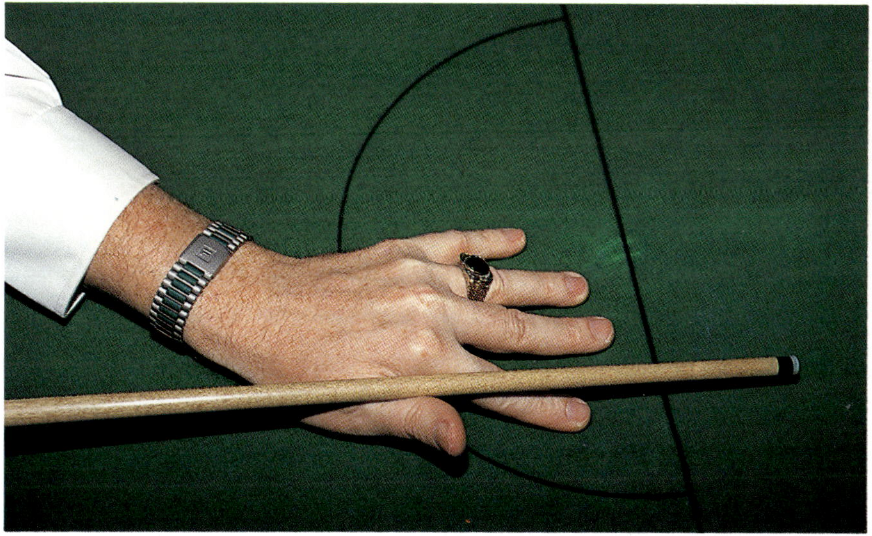

Rules of 9-ball pool

- The game is played on a rectangular six-pocket table with nine balls plus a cue ball. Balls comprise numerical balls numbered 1–9 plus the cue ball.

- The player legally pocketing the 9-ball, either after pocketing all the numerical balls in rotation or by a combination shot, after first hitting the lowest numbered ball on the table, wins the game.

- The balls are racked as shown in fig. 12 with the 1-ball on the 1-ball spot, which is at the intersection of the centre and corner pockets, with the 9-ball in the centre of the diamond. The other object balls are placed at random within the diamond.

- The opening player must hit the 1-ball from the break. The cue ball is played from any position on or within the 'D'. He must pocket a ball or cause at least two object balls to hit a cushion. Failure to do so is a foul break and will result in the balls being re-racked. The opposing player re-starts.

- If the player pockets the 9-ball from a legal break, he will win the game. If the player pockets the 9-ball from a foul break, the balls will be re-racked and the opposing player re-starts the game.

- A player must always hit the lowest numbered ball on the table with the cue ball on the first impact; failing to do so is a foul.

- Following any foul, except for a foul break, the opponent may play the cue ball from any position on the table or ask the offending player to play again.

- A player potting the 9-ball and the cue ball on the same shot will lose the game, except following a foul break.

- A player potting the 9-ball, after failing to first hit the lowest ball on the table, will lose the game.

- A player making three consecutive fouls will lose the game.

- The game is completed when the 9-ball is potted, in any pocket, and all the remaining balls have come to rest, except following a foul break.

- **Guidance:** (i) following a foul the player does not have two visits; (ii) if a legal shot cannot be played, the player must still play a shot, the only penalty being a foul.

▲ *Fig. 12 Racking of balls for 9-ball pool*

Other pool games

Speed pool

Objective
To pot all the balls in the fastest time.

Racking
As for basic pool.

Competition
(1) Players enter their names in any space available in *one* of any 'heat'.
(2) Players have three goes in finding their fastest time, and write their time for each go in the boxes by their name for their heat.
(3) In each heat, players can either have their three goes consecutively, or we recommend that each player plays alternately.
(4) When all players have had their three goes in a heat, the fastest time is the heat winner.
(5) The four heat winners then compete to decide the champion.

Rules
(1) Nominate a time-keeper for the frame.
(2) Once the time-keeper says go, the clock starts ticking. When the last ball is potted, the clock stops.
(3) The player can pot any ball in any order (including black).
(4) If the cue ball is potted or comes off the table, it is re-spotted in the 'D'.
(5) If any other ball comes off the table it is re-spotted on the head spot or as near to it as possible in a line from the head spot to the centre of the 'D'.
(6) Only the player on the table may pick up and replace balls as in (4) and (5) above; his penalty is the time taken to do this.
(7) In the event of a tie, the players concerned have one go each until there is a winner.

Best shot competition

Objective
To pot all the balls using the least number of shots.

Racking
As for basic pool.

How to play
(1) Over three frames; count for each frame the number of shots taken to pot all balls in any order. Your lowest score is used to decide your position. (Ask a friend to keep score.)
(2) There are four heats; enter in one only.
(3) When all names are entered on to the match sheet, commence the competition.
(4) Each of the heat winners will play off to find out who is really the best shot.
(5) Any tie – play a deciding frame.

On the green (nine balls)

Objective
To pot a ball in each pocket with the lowest number of strokes.

Racking
White ball in 'D', *one* other ball on the centre spot (the 'tee').

How to play
(1)

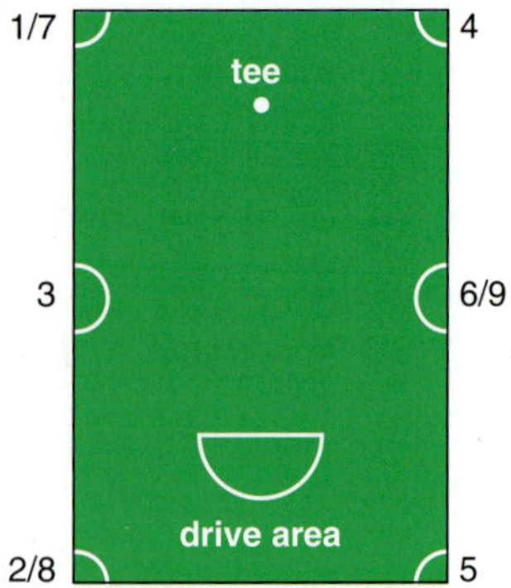

first green = holes 1–3
second green = holes 4–6
home run = holes 7–9

(2) **First putter (player)** Start on the first green; place one ball on the tee and putt (pot) into hole number 1, then the next ball on the tee to hole number 2 and then on to hole number 3. Move then to the second green, starting at hole number 4, then number 5 and then number 6. You putt the last three balls (the home run) starting at hole number 7 and ending at hole number 9.
(3) **In the 'rough' (foul)** If you pocket the white – add a stroke to your score. If you putt into the wrong hole – add three strokes to your score. If you run out of balls for your remaining holes – add five strokes to your score for each hole that you cannot putt a ball into.
(4) When all nine balls are putted, add up your strokes and then the next putter putts.
(5) **Tie** Play for hole number 3 – one ball per player; the lowest score wins.

Winner
Whoever has the lowest score.

◀ *Fig. 13 On the green* *Fig. 14 Golf* ▶

Golf (nine balls)

Objective
To pot a ball in each pocket within the allowed number of 'goes' ('par').

Racking
In a diamond, in any order.

How to play
(1) Each hole has a number of 'goes' allowed, i.e. par.

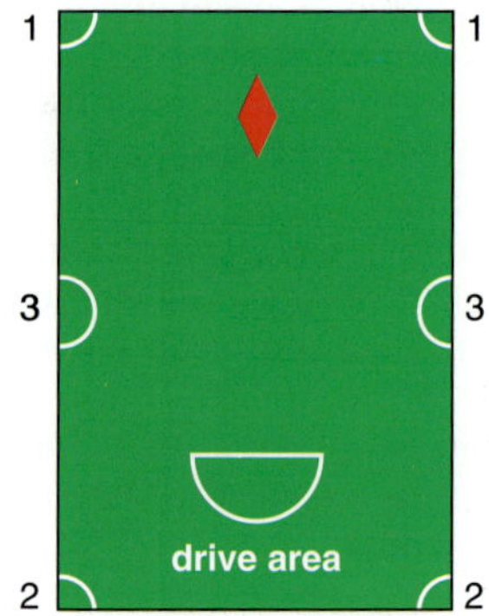

table par value = 18

(2) Golf balls are putted (potted) in any order. However, you nominate each ball for the pocket and must putt it in that pocket. Start on the first green with par 1 pockets, then on to par 2 pockets, and then par 3 pockets; then on to the second green.
(3) When six balls have been putted, pocket the last three – each in a different par pocket.
(4) **In the 'rough' (foul)** If you pocket the white – add a stroke to your score. If you putt into the wrong hole – add the par value to your score. If you run out of balls for your remaining holes up to ball number 6 – use the hole par value as your score; for balls 7, 8 and 9 – add three per ball plus the whole par value as your score.
(5) After the first golfer has potted nine balls, then golfer number two starts. Take the table par value from your total number of strokes to get your net score.

Winner
The golfer with the lowest net score.

Diamond nine (nine balls)

Objective
Pot number 1 first, then number 2, etc., and number 9 last.

Racking
Rack the balls in a diamond shape with number 9 in the middle, number 1 at the front, and the white ball in the 'D'.

How to play
(1) Hit the lowest numbered ball first – if pocketed, score 1 point; then try to pocket the next lowest numbered ball – if pocketed, one point, etc., until you fail to pocket the ball or make a *diamond Lil* (foul)!
(2) **Diamond Lil!** If you pocket or hit the wrong number, pot the white, or miss a ball completely, the next player places the white ball anywhere!
(3) **Scoring** One point for each correct ball, but whoever pockets the number 9 (if still on the table!) last gets an extra five points!

Winner
Whoever scores the most *points*.

Survivor

Objective
To be last remaining player on the table.

Racking
As for basic pool.

How to play
(1) Any number of players may enter.
(2) Players play alternatively.
(3) Each player has three 'lives'.
(4) A player on his turn has to pot a ball (any ball including the 8-ball black) – except the cue ball.
(5) Should a player fail to pot a ball, he loses a 'life'; if he loses all three 'lives' he is out.
(6) If a player pots the cue ball, goes in off, or causes a ball to leave the table, he loses a life.
(7) Any ball off the table is placed as near the head spot as possible; the cue ball is placed in the 'D'.
(8) When the last ball is potted and there is more than one survivor remaining, the balls are re-racked and the next player on breaks.
(9) At all times the player who breakes has an extra shot.

Index